LET'S RECYCLE GRANDAD

A COLLECTION OF BRILLIANT NEW AND RECYCLED POEMS

PAPER GLASS CANS POETRY

CHOSEN BY ROGER STEVENS

Illustrated by Nigel Baines

A & C Black • London

First published 2008 by
A & C Black Publishers Ltd
38 Soho Square, London, W1D 3HB

www.acblack.com

Collection copyright © 2008 Roger Stevens
Illustrations copyright © 2008 Nigel Baines

The rights of Roger Stevens and Nigel Baines to be identified as
the editor and illustrator of this work have been asserted by them in
accordance with the Copyrights, Designs and Patents Act 1988.

ISBN 978-0-7136-8851-1

A CIP catalogue for this book is available from the British Library.

This book is produced using paper that is made from wood grown in
managed, sustainable forests. It is natural, renewable and recyclable.
The logging and manufacturing processes conform to the
environmental regulations of the country of origin.

Printed and bound in Great Britain
by CPI Cox and Wyman, Reading, RG1 8EX.

CONTENTS

GOING GREEN

ANIMAL ESCAPADES

THINGS THAT GO BUMP IN THE NIGHT

PLAYING WITH WORDS

IT CAME FROM OUTER SPACE

STUFF AND NONSENSE

PAUSE FOR THOUGHT

THE LAST LAUGH

GOING GREEN

LET'S RECYCLE GRANDAD

Let's recycle Grandad
Make him much more squashy
Let's throw away his bony bits
And make him much more comfy

His shuffling and his stoop can go
We'll bin his wrinkles, too
Let's make him younger, fitter, faster
Rebuild him just like new

Let's recycle Grandad
But not his sunny smile
Let's not recycle his lovely hugs
Or his tales of being a child

Let's not recycle his funny jokes
They always lift the gloom
Let's not recycle his booming laugh
That bounces around the room

For those bits are the best bits
And ought to stay, in fact
Let's not recycle Grandad
Let's leave Grandad intact

Andrea Shavick & Roger Stevens

GRANDAD'S WILL

Though Grandad's gone he still lives on
His features not forgotten
For he's left Dad the face he had
And me – his windy bottom!

Justin Coe

MISS WISE ON HER BIKE

Fluorescent by day
Reflective by night
Miss Wise on her bike
Is a wonderful sight

She glides through the traffic
Freewheels past the jam
And all the time thinks
What a smart girl I am

I arrive on time
I don't pay to park
I'm soon at my desk
And ready to start

Then when my work's done
And it's time to go
I put on my helmet
My journey's not slow

When I take to the road
On the days I commute
I'm happy to say
I don't clog or pollute

Fluorescent by day
Reflective by night
Miss Wise on her bike
Is a wonderful sight

Bernard Young

WHO'S THERE?

Who's there?
Who's that hiding behind the brown trees,
lurking amongst the green undergrowth of
    the woodland?
It's us – the Tree-Elves and the Moss-People
and we are watching you
breaking branches without permission.

Who's there?
Who's that gliding over the wet rocks,
dancing and splashing at the sea's edge?
It's us – the Rock Sirens and Mer-men
and we are watching you
pouring poison into our watery home.

Who's there?
Who's that drifting through the sparkling
    mist,
flying across bright skies, bursting out of
    clouds?
It's us – the Alven, we who travel in bubbles
    of air
and we are watching you
filling our palace of sky with dust and dirt.

Who's there?
Who's that running over the mountains,
wading through cold rivers, striding over
    forests?
It's us – the Kelpies and Glashans,
the powerful beasts of the wiser world
and we are watching you
wasting these waters and hurting this land.

John Rice

PROGRESS

1
The yields
of fields
were cows and crops

but now
no cows
just streets and shops

2
A crocodile
will rarely smile
she knows your plans are drastic

She'll save her skin
with a mirthless grin –
and suggest you use some plastic

Trevor Millum

THIRTEEN WAYS TO RECYCLE AN OLD LOTTERY TICKET

Roll into a tooth-pick
Mop up mouse sick
Make an origami yeti
Cut to small bits for confetti
Make a mini carrier bag
Stick to pencil, use as flag
A bookmark in a Harry Potter
Make a fan for baby otter
Cover up satsuma stain
Make a paper aeroplane
Alternatively use as glider
For espresso, it's a coaster
Use as blanket to catch spider
Jumping from a burning toaster

Roger Stevens

THE GREEN UNICORN

He came with the storm.

On Monday,
he evaporated all weapons
as though they had never been invented.
On Tuesday,
he turned all cars and lorries
into bicycles and milk floats.

On Wednesday,
he destroyed all polluting factories
and he refreshed the air.
On Thursday,
he cleansed the lakes and the seas
and he breathed life into dead rivers.

On Friday,
he freed all zoo animals
and returned them to renewed homelands.
On Saturday,
he took a little from those that had much
and gave much to those that had little.

On Sunday,
he tried to share his love with every heart,
but he was weary
and couldn't be sure that he had reached
   them all.
He left with the wind,
and he whispered to the World,
"Now have another try."

Mike Jubb

I'M NOT SAYING

I'm not saying
My brother-in-law
Is environmentally
Unfriendly
But the grass
Is sparse
On the plot
Where we buried him

Matt Harvey

PLANET FOR SALE

In need of some repair
Six point seven billion careless owners
Lovely views of the galaxy
Possible renovation project

Owners seek an exchange
With similar elsewhere
In universe
Must have a sun
Plenty of money for
A shiny new model
With an ozone layer

Sue Hardy-Dawson

ENVIRONMENTALLY FRIENDLY HAIKU

To save energy
Not to mention trees and ink
I'll stop writing now

Andrea Shavick

ANIMAL
ESCAPADES

GOT THE HUMP

Gran says
if she were a witch
she'd turn our cat
(who's grumpy,
who's always got the hump)
into a camel.

I'd like that.
No one else
in our street
has a camel flap.

Joan Poulson

DOG'S DITTY

In the park after dark
Minibeasts have midnight feasts:
Moths spread cloths for fireflies
And share their tasty pollen pies.

But in the park after dark
All I do is bark and bark;
Bark and bark and bark and bark
And bark and bark and
B A R K !

Celia Warren

BUTTERFLY

On wings flake-fragile,
petal-frail, you somehow sail,
long mile after mile.

Kate Williams

MOBILE HOME FOR SALE

Judy is a delightful
Mobile Home
with Central Heating
a warm Basement
superb Penthouse Views
and includes luxury
Deep Pile Carpets
in black and white.
Fully Air-Conditioned
by large wagging tail.
This Border Collie
would suit large family of fleas.

Roger Stevens

ESCAPADES

I have no luck with pets...
I had a rabbit
but he hopped it.
I had a worm
but it wriggled away.
I had a horse
but he hoofed it.
And my stick insect
wouldn't stick around.
I had a cow
but she moo...ved on.
I had a snake
but it slipped away.
I had a bat
but it flitted.
And my antelope
...eloped.
I had a greyhound
but it did a runner.
Even my bees buzzed off.
My lady-like ladybird
flew away home.
And my moose
...vamooosed
My fleas fled.
My flies flew.

My birds took wing.
My kangaroo took a homeward bound.
Even my sloth wouldn't hang around.
So now I've decided
no more pets for me.
Pets are too much bother.
If I want a smelly creature round the house
I'll settle for my baby brother.

Michaela Morgan

THE LAST TASMANIAN TIGER

It roared as it roamed the small cage
And people all hurried to see
They pushed and shoved at each other
While the tiger just wished it could flee.

The last Tasmanian tiger
Stared open-mouthed at me
I looked back through the bars of the cage
And imagined when it was free.

The search for another continues
And everyone's making a fuss
But maybe it's best we don't find it
Maybe it's hiding from us.

Celina Macdonald

THE SNAKE'S REVENGE

You could never imagine me,
not in a zillion years,
I'm far beyond the scope of
your wildest nightmares or fears.

But I'm here, at the edge of your universe,
a creature of immeasurable girth.
Hatred has made me huge, and now
I'm the snake that will swallow the Earth.

And I'm moving even closer,
I've already gobbled up stars,
I've unhinged my jaws and soon I'll be ready
to take a crack at Mars.

And when I finally reach you
I'll tell you what I'll do
I shall wrap my coils around your planet
and squeeze the breath out of you.

And this will be my revenge
from the time that I was cursed,
for eternity spent on my belly,
for the dust that I ate, for my thirst.

And remember well, if you will,
for a snake is nobody's friend,

I was there at the very beginning
and I'll be there at the end.

For the world won't finish in flame
or by drowning in a flood.
It won't be wholly engulfed
in an ocean of angry mud.

There'll be no explosion, no fracture,
no tremors from a last earthquake.
I tell you now, this world will end
in the belly of a snake.

Brian Moses

THINGS THAT GO BUMP IN THE NIGHT

IS IT HUNTING YOU?

At dead of night, when the moon is full
it prowls across the moor.
Its fangs are bared, its eyes throb red.
What is it hunting for?

The air is still. Its chilling howls
echo back in time.
Against the moon, its silhouette
sends shivers down your spine.

It's closer now. Don't try to hide,
there's nothing you can do.
It's on its way and you are doomed
if *it* is hunting *you*.

Jane Clarke

SCARY NIGHT

On Hallowe'en night, as she smoothed my
　　bedspread,
My mum saw me shivering, and here's what
　　she said:
"Forget all those stories you've heard and
　　you've read.
Now, why don't you lie down and sleep tight
　　instead?
No creatures'll get you. You've nothing to
　　dread."
My dad stood beside her and nodded his
　　head...
And so did the witch as she flew overhead
And so did the monster from under my bed
And so did the werewolf who looked
　　underfed
And so did the zombie, although kind of dead
And so did our neighbours, as each of them
　　fled
And so did the vampire, as his victim bled
And so did his victim whose neck was all red
And me, I just shivered beneath my
　　bedspread
And thought of the stories I'd heard and I'd
　　read.

Nick Toczek

THE NEW GIRL

The new girl stood at Miss Moon's desk,
Her face pale as a drawing
On white paper
Her lips coloured too heavily
With a too-dark crayon.

When the others shouted, "Me! Me!"
I curled my fists,
Tried not to think of friendship,
Or whispered secrets,
Or games for two players.
But the empty seat beside me
Shimmered with need
And my loneliness dragged her like a magnet.

As she sat down
I caught the musty smell of old forests,
Noticed the threads that dangled
At her thin wrists,
The purple stitches that circled
Her swan's neck.
Yet I loved her quietness,
The way she held her pencil
Like a feather,
The swooping curves of her name,
The dreaminess of her cold eyes.

At night, I still wonder
Where she sleeps,
If she sleeps,
And what Miss Moon will say
To her tattered parents
On Open Day.

Clare Bevan

THE OLD CURIOSITY SHOP

I opened the door and walked right on in
And found myself back on the outside again
I peered through the window and what did
    I see?
Myself – looking back from the inside at me!

I went round the back and knocked on
    the door
Something knocked back, and then gave a
    roar
I peeked through the letterbox, and to my
    surprise
I was staring straight into three bloodshot
    eyes.

I ran all the way home like a dog from a trap
And woke up my dad who was having a nap
"I remember that shop," he said with a
    frown.
"About ten years ago – they pulled the place
    down!"

Michael Leigh

THE JELLY BONE MAN

The jelly bone man
oozes through the cracks.
Folds himself up
and disappears
into his own hollow heart.
When he comes
to wrap you in a hug,
the sleeves of his coat,
lapels of his jacket,
flap around you –
swallow you up
in a great gulp gulf.
Then he'll spin around
spin... spin – like a terrible top,
until his arms are empty
and his smile is wide open
and his eyes gleam cold as space.
And you?
You'll be gone.
Gone...
Gone...
Into the nothing
the dizzy dark nothing
of the jelly bone...

                      ... jelly bone man.

Jan Dean

A HALLOWE'EN CHARM FOR SWEET DREAMS

May the ghost
   lie in its grave.
May the vampire
   see the light.
May the witch
   keep to her cave.
And the spectre
   melt from sight.

May the wraith
    stay in the wood.
May the banshee
    give no fright.
May the ghoul
    be gone for good.
And the zombie
    haste in flight.

May the troll
    no more be seen.
May the werewolf
    lose its bite.
May all the spooks
    and children green
Fade forever

    in

        the

            night...

Wes Magee

WONDERFUL PUPIL

It's lovely to meet you at last
  Mrs Dracula
Your son is a wonderful pupil

He's very good at science
Especially the study of blood

He did a beautiful drawing in art
Of a bat

He was top in history and geography
He's very knowledgeable
About Transylvania, isn't he?

You and Mr Dracula
Must be very proud.

Where is Mr Dracula?
Oh, he'll be along later
When it gets dark.

Jolly good,
I'm looking forward
To meeting him.

Roger Stevens

PLAYING
WITH WORDS

THERE'S A POEM

In your granny's apple crumble there's
    a poem
In a beggar's mumbled stumble there's
    a poem
In the bumble of a bee
In the jungle of the sea
And in the rumble of your tummy there's
    a poem
When your tongue is tied there's a poem
When your dog has died there's a poem
Or if your backside is too wide
For a ride down the slide
And you've no pride left to hide there's
    a poem
In the fog of your brains there's a poem
Turn the cog, release the chains there's
    a poem
When a copper on a chopper
Tries to stop a hot spacehopper
But on the corner comes a cropper there's
    a poem
And when the wind is blowing and the
    trees are to and fro-ing
And when the grass is growing and one
    man goes a-mowing
And when from a long throw in the ball
    falls to Michael Owen

And he gets a toe in but the ball it doesn't
  go in
And the frustration is showing there's a...
  punch-up!

In everything you hear there's a poem
Out in the atmosphere there's a poem
Sometimes you think there isn't
But if you look a little differently
And listen really carefully there's a poem

Justin Coe

PROFESSIONAL WRITER

I'm a professional writer
Today I wrote the word "Mother"
I've refilled my pencil
And sharpened my pen —
So tomorrow I may write another

Ian Billings

WHAT POETS EAT FOR LUNCH

Around one o'clock, when they're ready for
    lunch,
poets decide on which sandwich to munch.
Some always go for fillings that rhyme,
forgetting that taste should come first every
    time.
So lamb may be chosen with soft bits of clam
or ham thickly smothered with cranberry jam.
A bap or a wrap with slivers of gammon
with frogs' legs, ducks' eggs and the roe of
    a salmon.
Salami, pastrami and a nice bit of brisket,
fat from a rat and a sprinkling of biscuit.
Lychees and cheese with a garnish of fleas –
all the above are quite likely to please.

Other poets, time after time,
choose alliterative fillings, rather than rhyme.
So tiny tomatoes, tuna and tongue,
lugworms and lentils with lemon and lung,
Brussels, baloney, bananas and beet –
any of these would be right up their street.

Mind you, some are less fickle,
liking pickle and free verse.

Trevor Parsons

THE HAIKU MONSTER

The haiku monster
Gobbles up the syllables
Crunching words and CHOMP!

The haiku monster
Slurps the s in paghetti
Bites bs for reakfast

The haiku monster
Jumbles all the telrets pu
Makes   disappear

The haiku monster
Nibbles on the v w ls nd
Chews consonants

The haiku monster,
Alphabet joker, plays with
The lettuce and the worms

The haiku monster
Hides rude words in the poem
And spoils bum snog vest

Mixes up the lines
The haiku monster
Ruining the layout

Paul Cookson

A POEM WITH TWO LAURAS IN IT

"Laura, is that you?"
"Yes, Laura, it's me."
"Where are we?"
"We're caught inside some sort of three-
    verse poem."
"POEM?"
"Look out! Here comes the second verse.
Jump!"

"Made it."
"Now that we're in this poem, what do we
    do?"
"Maybe we should rhyme for a bit."
"We'd have to find the words to fit."
"Good. That worked. Think of something,
    Laura."
"My jumper. It's made from angora."
"Phew. Lucky you weren't wearing your
    sweatshirt."
"Mum wouldn't let me. It was covered with
    dirt."
"I wish this verse would come to an end."
"This rhyming is driving me round the bend."
"Look below you. It's verse number three."
"I'll go first. You follow me."

"That was a near thing. I'm exhausted."

"Me too.
Let's rest on this long line until the poem
  comes to an end."

John Coldwell

WHIPPING UP A STORM

Storm's coming
air's humming
thunder's drumming
mumbling under breath
and grumbling.
Storm's coming
closer, closer
nosing through those
open windows
floating, hot ghost
boasting
then it flings
cool air like wings
giant things
almost sings
then is beating
flapping sheeting
cool air greeting
meeting
sweeping in
the lacy raindrops
spotting
hopping, dropping
jumping, plopping
in the street.
Listen to the beat
all around your feet –

everywhere they meet
flooding, mudding
bubble sudding
and the bass drum
thunder comes
dumping tons of rain
and thumping once again.
Here comes the rain
rain rain rain
slowing, slowly going
going slow.
Now no
no rain.

Jill Townsend

WHAT SHALL I CALL IT?

I need a name for this poem
Has anyone got a clue?
It needs to be funny, slightly surreal
You know, seen from an odd point of view

For example – Low-flying Rabbits Ahead
Beware – High-flying Hares
Aardvark Through the Looking Glass
Why the Wow Wow Got Stuck on the Stairs

I Fell in Love with a Ynambu
Grabbing a Tamarin's Tail
Waiting for the Quetzal
Playing Hide and Seek with a Whale

The Fiddler Spider's Party
When the Cheetah Raced the Sloth
There's a Halibut in the Underpass
Two Many Coypu Spoil the Broth

The Twelve Starfish of the Zodiac
The Secret of Prairie Dog's Box
Why Alligators love Elevators
Why Otters Don't Wear Socks

I could try The Cry of the Corncrake
Or maybe the Plea of the Moose

Perhaps The Petulant Puttock
Or There's an Amoeba on the Loose

I need a name for this poem
What to call it – I haven't a clue
I think I'll just call it – What Shall I Call It?
And leave the decision to you

Roger Stevens

BOURBONS

My little brother thought
That the scary ladies
With evil eyes
And snakes in their hair
Were called
Bourbons.

So

Whenever our aunties
Asked us round for tea,
We would cover our faces
And shout:
"DON'T LOOK AT THE BISCUITS –
THEY'LL TURN YOU TO STONE!"

And our angry aunties
Would glare at us
Like GORGONS.

Clare Bevan

IT CAME FROM
OUTER SPACE

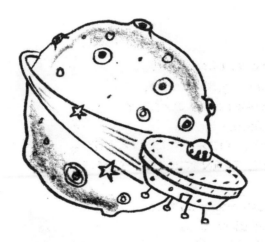

EVENING SHIFTS

As cloak-black clouds
Of evening drift
Across his torch-white eye.

The moon begins
His evening shift –
Night-watchman of the sky.

Graham Denton

MOON THEORY

Some scientists set out to prove
the moon is made of cheese;
the evidence they discover means
that everyone agrees

The crusty surface of the moon
has bubbled into craters
caused, they think, by heating cheese
that's been through giant graters.

Now satisfied that they are right,
the scientists can boast
that, some day soon, they're sure to find
a planet made of toast...

Celia Warren

CATCH

I caught the sun today
But you should have seen the star
That got away

Matt Harvey

NEIL ARMSTRONG

(A clerihew)

Neil Armstrong
Wasn't on the moon for long.
But in that time he left behind
A giant footprint for mankind.

John Foster

IS ANYONE ELSE OUT THERE?

Sometimes at night, in my garden,
I lie on my back, and I stare
At the billions of stars, and I wonder
Is anyone else out there?
And somewhere in space, I imagine,
There's a Being whose thoughts I share:
As he lies on his back, and he wonders
Is anyone else out there?

Mike Jubb

MY ROCKET

My rocket's got lots of levers,
My rocket's got lots of springs,
My rocket's got lots of nuts and bolts
And shiny metal things.

It's got dials with lines and numbers,
And lights that blink and burn,
It's got things that bang and buzz and beep,
And knobs to twist and turn.

It can play all sorts of music,
And tune to kids' TV,
It can drill through rocks and wash my socks
And cook baked beans for tea.

It can bake great buns and do huge sums,
But the thing I haven't found
Is the rocket knob that will do the job
Of getting it off the ground.

Julia Rawlinson

WHO KNOWS ABOUT UFOS?

If UFOs are Unidentified Flying Objects –
whose job is it to identify them?

And, once identified, does a UFO become
   an IFO?

And, if a UFO can no longer fly –
perhaps due to a technical problem –
does it become a UO?

And, if I threw my slipper in the air –
and nobody knew what it was –
would it too be a UFO?

I think I'll file these questions under
Utterly Fantastic Observations.

James Carter

SNACK ATTACK

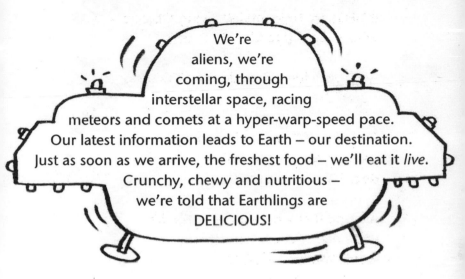

We're
aliens, we're
coming, through
interstellar space, racing
meteors and comets at a hyper-warp-speed pace.
Our latest information leads to Earth – our destination.
Just as soon as we arrive, the freshest food – we'll eat it *live*.
Crunchy, chewy and nutritious –
we're told that Earthlings are
DELICIOUS!

Liz Brownlee

BLACK HOLE

A giant plughole out in space, it swirls down suns without a trace. It takes entire galaxies, without a by-your-leave or please, and fits all in no need to squeeze. You may not want to read this verse, for I'm afraid that it gets worse – there's room for the universe. There's no plug big enough I fear, so in some distant, future year, we're all going to disappear...

Liz Brownlee

SPACE HAS NO CEILING

Space has no ceiling, no walls, no floor,
no gate to go through to see what's next
  door.

There's nothing to measure; no big, no
  small –
nothing to climb up, nowhere to fall.

Space has no colours; no green, blue or
  pink –
apart from the stars, it's all black as ink.

There's no sound, no noise, no voice to hear,
no music beyond the atmosphere.

Infinity – that's what space does best.
But our little Earth has all the rest.

Kate Williams

SONNET FOR A SPHERE

Take an apple. Chop it into quarters.
Count out three. These represent the lakes
that nestle inside countries, all the snaking
rivers joined with seas – the blue that's water.

Put them aside. This last remaining slice
stands for the land. Divide it into eight.
Discard the barren: the distant icy waste,
the thirsty desert, rocky unreached heights.

What's left? Just one last sliver of a sphere.
Unpeel its skin. Hold up that patch of green
between your thumb and fingertip. It's here
the soil is rich and seeds take root. The crops
we need to harvest, where our livestock feed
are all in this. Be careful now – don't drop it.

Rachel Rooney

STUFF AND NONSENSE

SUNDAY IN THE YARM FARD

The mat keowed
The mow cooed
The bog darked
The kigeon pooed

The squicken chalked
The surds bang
The kwuk dacked
The burch rells chang

And then, after all the dacking and the
  changing
The chalking and the banging
The darking and the pooing
The keowing and the cooing
There was a mewtiful beaumont
Of queace and pie-ate

Trevor Millum

THE METAMORPHOSIS OF
MR MCARTHUR

Nine o'clock, he took the register, as usual.
But instead of sitting up straight and glaring,
hissing out names in strict alphabetical order,
he leapt onto the desk and screeched each
  name
so loud, our eardrums sang. By nine fifteen
we hadn't even started Literacy Hour.
He threw our books at us
and went off into a corner to scratch.

By ten o'clock – we didn't like to say, but
man! He was hairy! Great dark tufts of it
all over his hands and face and neck.
He ripped open his shirt and his chest
was furrier than our dog.
His lips ballooned, his nostrils
stretched like entrances to two dark caves.
His eyes shone black as briefcases
and a tail trailed out of his trouser leg.

At break-time, he hogged the climbing frame,
pushed everyone else off
and shoved his bum in Mrs Andrews' face
when she tugged his sleeve.
I must admit, his ability to hang
by one long clawed hand, and swing

was something we hadn't realised
about Mr McArthur.

That day we did no spelling, art, maths
or science. He climbed out of the window,
beckoned us to follow him,
and we jumped from ledge to ledge,
shrieking, and beating our chests. It was fun,
and only three people went to hospital.
Mr McArthur waved them off,
jumping up and down, and eating a banana.

Mr McArthur doesn't teach us any more.
Our new teacher, Miss Price, has skin
as smooth and clammy as a fish and shows
no interest in scaling the building.
She gives us extra homework and tells us
we're not taking school seriously enough.
Mr McArthur giggles when we pass him at
  home-time,
as he hangs off the school gates, upside
  down.

Catherine Smith

TO A VERY SPECIAL SLOPE

You're such a radiant gradient
A smooth one, not a hilly one
Your red-rimmed sign says you're one-in-nine
But to me you're one in a million

Matt Harvey

NO BREAD

I wish I'd made a list
I forgot to get the bread.
If I forget it again
I'll be dead.

We had blank and butter pudding,
beans on zip.
Boiled egg with deserters,
no chip butty: just chip.

I wish I'd made a list
I forgot to get the bread.
My mam got the empty bread bin
and wrapped it round my head.

Our jam sarnies were just jam
floating on the air.
We spread butter on the table
cos the bread wasn't there.

My mam says if I run away
she knows I won't be missed.
Not like the bread was...
I wish I'd made a list!

Ian McMillan

SMOKE ALARM

during the night
our Smoke Alarm went off
and off and off and off and off
and off and off and off and off
and off and off and off and off
and off and off and off and off
and off and off and off and off

until Dad hit it with his shoe

Steven Herrick

THE TROUBLE WITH GERANIUMS

The trouble with geraniums
Is that they're much too red
The trouble with my toast is that
It's far too full of bread

The trouble with a diamond
Is that it's much too bright
The same applies to fish and stars
And the electric light

The trouble with the stars I see
Lies in the way they fly
The trouble with myself is all
Self-centred in the eye

The trouble with my looking-glass
Is that it shows me, me;
There's trouble in all sorts of things
Where it should never be.

Mervyn Peake

HULA HOOPING

My little brother hula hoops,
He hula hoops all day,
He hula hoops before sun's up,
And after it's away.

My little brother hula hoops,
Around his every limb,
But suddenly I realise that,
His hula's hooping him.

Violet Macdonald

MIDNIGHT FEAST

There was an old man from Peru
Who dreamed he was eating his shoe
He woke in a fright
In the middle of the night
And found out it was perfectly true.

Anon

PAUSE FOR THOUGHT

DROP IN THE OCEAN

Sloshing around
in life's restless sea,
there's a drop in the ocean –
and that drop is me.

Riding the waves,
or washed up on the shore,
I'm a miniscule drop
amongst zillions more.

I'm a drop in the ocean
of life's restless sea –
but there'd be no ocean
without drops like me.

Jane Clarke

HOW BIG IS A FACT?

How big is a fact?
I need to know,
I'm worried that
My head will grow –
Each time I learn
Another figure
I'm sure my brain
Gets slightly bigger.

Teachers keep teaching
Week by week,
I hear my skull
Begin to creak,
And already my head
Is tightly packed,
So I need to know,
How big is a fact?

Julia Rawlinson

WILD!

Wild the garden overgrown
wild the jaw that breaks the bone

Wild the rain that soaks the sand
wild the sun that cracks the land

Wild the summer's green and greed
wild the wind that sows the seed

Wild the flower, big in bloom
wild the early dawning tune

Wild the bird that seeks the sun
wild the cry when life is done

Wild the claw that rips the skin
wild the bite, the tear, the sting

Wild the young that feed to grow
wild the blood that stains the snow

Wild the stench of fresh decay
wild the mulch that rots away

Wild the thorn, the fruit, the bud
wild the roots, the shoots, the mud

Wild the song, the forest hum
wild the rhythm in the drum

Wild the honey in the comb
wild the hunter heading home

Wild the worm that breaks the soil
wild the world in constant toil

Wild the weed that lives in cracks
wild the scythe, the saw, the axe

Wild the heart at trees laid bear
wild that wild no longer there

James Carter

FANTASIA

I dream
of
giving birth
to
a child
who will ask,
Mother,
what was war?

Eve Merriam

THE OLDER THE VIOLIN THE SWEETER THE TUNE

Me Granny old
Me Granny wise
stories shine like a moon
from inside she eyes.

Me Granny can dance
Me Granny can sing
but she can't play violin.

Yet she always saying,
"Dih older dih violin
de sweeter de tune."

Me granny must be wiser
than the man inside the moon.

John Agard

GRANDAD'S FLOWERS

Those flowers
Pink, with daisy faces
Came from Grandad's.
He grew them from seeds
In his greenhouse,
Looked after them like babies,
Loved them,
Loved flowers and football and special toffee.

The toffee's gone,
The team's been relegated,
But in the garden
Grandad's flowers grow.

Daphne Kitching

SOMETHING TO DO IN A TRAFFIC JAM

Dream of
a world where bat
and tiger wander free
and turtles set their courses by
the stars.

Judith Nicholls

A PRAYER FOR PEACE

I wrote it
on the ocean waves
beneath a sheet
of sky.

It floated
on a rippling page
then rose on wings
to fly.

It fell and sank
to oily depths
where dolphins sing
and swim

beneath the tanks
and fighter jets
that tear through prayer
and hymn.

Celia Gentles

THE LAST
LAUGH

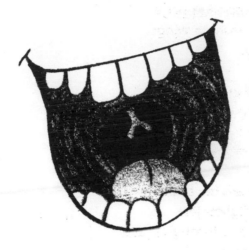

MY SISTER

My sister's remarkably light,
She can float to a fabulous height.
It's a troublesome thing,
But we tie her with string,
And we use her instead of a kite.

Margaret Mahy

FISHING

There is a fine
line

between fishing
and standing
on the bank
like
an idiot.

Gerard Benson

WORM WORDS

"Keep still,"
said Big Worm
to Little Worm.
"You're driving me
round the bend."

"Don't be daft,"
said Little Worm.
"I'm your other end."

Tony Mitton

CREATIVE DIFFERENCES

My grandma fills her hours
Painting plants and flowers
But Grandpa's not a very happy fellow

His geraniums are dead
After being painted red
And his bluebells don't look good when they
are yellow.

Linda Knaus

DEAD CHOKED

Freddie's Frog
leapt down his throat,
got stuck and
made him hoarse.
He glugged and gurgled,
coughed and choked –
but in the end
he croaked, of course.

Liz Brownlee

COOL AT THE POOL

Roll my muscles
Round the swimming pool
Make the girls goggle
Feel real cool

Flex my pecs
Swagger and pose
Look real tough
Look down my nose

Walk to the deep end
They all stare
My red shiny trunks
My real trendy hair

Stand on the diving board
Think I'll jump in
Just one problem
I can't swim

David Harmer

ARK ANGLERS

Noah let his sons go fishing
Only on the strictest terms:
Sit still, keep quiet and concentrate,
We've only got two worms!

Celia Warren

PRAYER

Let me walk in the fields and the forest
In a land that is rich and fair
Let me swim in the cool, clean ocean
Let me breathe untainted air

Let the sun's rays warm my body
Let the sun's light into my soul
Let us pray for this damaged planet
That one day it will heal and be whole

Roger Stevens

ACKNOWLEDGEMENTS

All poems have been included with kind permission of the authors.

'Grandad's Flowers' was first published in *Spider-flavoured Sausages*, poems by Daphne Kitching, Hands-Up Books, 2004

'Catch' and 'To a Very Special Slope' first appeared in *The Hole in the Sum of My Parts*, The Poetry Trust, 2005

'Neil Armstrong' was first published in *The Poetry Chest*, Oxford University Press, 2007

'Who's There?' was first published in *Bears Don't Like Bananas*, Simon and Schuster, 1991

'The New Girl' was first published in *Spooky Schools*, ed. Brian Moses, Macmillan, 2004

'Bourbons' was first published in *Hubble Bubble*, ed. Andrew Fusek Peters, Hodder Wayland, 2003